September 2012

HEALTH CARE FRAUD

Types of Providers Involved in Medicare, Medicaid, and the Children's Health Insurance Program Cases

GAO
Accountability * Integrity * Reliability

Highlights

Highlights of GAO-12-820, a report to congressional requesters

Why GAO Did This Study

GAO has designated Medicare and Medicaid—which are administered by the Centers for Medicare & Medicaid Services (CMS), an agency of HHS—as high-risk programs partly because their size and complexity make them vulnerable to fraud. Several federal agencies conduct health care fraud investigations and related activities, including HHS-OIG and DOJ's Civil Division, and the 93 U.S. Attorney's Offices (USAO). In fiscal year 2011, the federal government devoted at least $608 million to conduct such activities. Additionally, state MFCUs investigate health care fraud in their state's Medicaid and CHIP programs.

GAO was asked to provide information on the types of providers that are the subjects of fraud cases. This report identifies provider types who were the subjects of fraud cases in (1) Medicare, Medicaid, and CHIP that were handled by federal agencies, and changes in the types of providers in 2005 and 2010; and (2) Medicaid and CHIP fraud cases that were handled by MFCUs. To identify subjects of fraud cases handled by federal agencies, GAO combined data from three agency databases—HHS-OIG, USAOs, and DOJ's Civil Division—and removed duplicate subject data. GAO also reviewed public court records, such as indictments, to identify subjects' provider types because the USAOs and DOJ Civil Division data did not consistently include provider type. To describe providers involved in fraud cases handled by the MFCUs, GAO collected aggregate data from 10 state MFCUs, which represented the majority of fraud investigations, indictments, and convictions nationwide.

View GAO-12-820. For more information, contact Kathleen M. King at (202) 512-7114 or kingk@gao.gov.

What GAO Found

According to 2010 data from the Department of Health and Human Services' Office of the Inspector General (HHS-OIG) and the Department of Justice (DOJ), 10,187 subjects—individuals and entities involved in fraud cases—were investigated for health care fraud, including fraud in Medicare, Medicaid, and the Children's Health Insurance Program (CHIP). These subjects included different types of providers and suppliers—such as physicians, hospitals, durable medical equipment suppliers, home health agencies, and pharmacies—that serve Medicare, Medicaid, and CHIP beneficiaries. For criminal cases in 2010, medical facilities—including medical centers, clinics, or practices—and durable medical equipment suppliers were the most-frequent subjects investigated. Hospitals and medical facilities were the most-frequent subjects investigated in civil fraud cases, including cases that resulted in judgments or settlements.

- **Subjects of criminal cases**: Many of the 7,848 criminal subjects in 2010 were medical facilities or durable medical equipment suppliers, representing about 40 percent of subjects of criminal cases. Similarly, in 2005, medical facilities and durable medical equipment suppliers accounted for 41 percent of criminal case subjects. Data from 2010 show that most of the subjects were in cases that were not referred by HHS-OIG to DOJ for prosecution (85 percent). Of the subjects whose cases were pursued, most were found guilty or pled guilty or no contest.

- **Subjects of civil cases**: Over one-third of the 2,339 subjects of civil cases in 2010 were hospitals and medical facilities. In 2010, about 35 percent more subjects were investigated in civil fraud cases than in 2005. Nearly half of the subjects of 2010 cases were pursued. Among the subjects whose cases were pursued, 55 percent resulted in judgments or settlements.

Additionally, data from HHS-OIG show that nearly 2,200 individuals and entities were excluded from program participation for health care fraud convictions and other reasons, including license revocation and program-related convictions. About 60 percent of those individuals and entities excluded were in the nursing profession. Pharmacies or individuals affiliated with pharmacies were the next-largest provider type excluded, representing about 7 percent of those excluded.

According to data GAO collected from 10 state Medicaid Fraud Control Units (MFCU), over 40 percent of the 2,742 subjects investigated for health care fraud in Medicaid and CHIP in 2010 were home health care providers and health care practitioners. Of the criminal cases pursued by these MFCUs, home health care providers comprised nearly 40 percent of criminal convictions and 45 percent of subjects sentenced in 2010. Civil health care fraud cases pursued by these MFCUs in 2010 resulted in judgments and settlements totaling nearly $829 million. Pharmaceutical manufacturers were to pay more than 60 percent ($509 million) of the total amount of civil judgments and settlements.

GAO provided a draft of the report to DOJ and HHS. DOJ provided technical comments, which have been incorporated as appropriate.

_____ United States Government Accountability Office

Contents

Abbreviations

CHIP	Children's Health Insurance Program
CMS	Centers for Medicare & Medicaid Services
DOJ	Department of Justice
EOUSA	Executive Office of U.S. Attorneys
FCA	False Claims Act
FBI	Federal Bureau of Investigation
HHS	Department of Health and Human Services
HHS-OIG	Department of Health and Human Services' Office of Inspector General
MFCU	Medicaid Fraud Control Unit
PACER	Public Access to Court Electronic Records
PPACA	Patient Protection and Affordable Care Act
USAO	U.S. Attorney's Office

United States Government Accountability Office
Washington, DC 20548

September 7, 2012

The Honorable Harry Reid
Majority Leader
United States Senate

The Honorable Max Baucus
Chairman
Committee on Finance
United States Senate

The Honorable Tom Harkin
Chairman
Committee on Health, Education, Labor, and Pensions
United States Senate

In fiscal year 2011, 48.4 million individuals were enrolled in Medicare; 55.6 million in Medicaid; and 8.7 million in the Children's Health Insurance Program (CHIP).[1] Together, these programs accounted for approximately $849.2 billion in federal expenditures.[2] The federal government allocated at least $608 million in funding to investigate and prosecute cases of alleged health care fraud in health care programs that year.[3] Many different types of providers and suppliers who serve Medicare, Medicaid,

---

[1]The Centers for Medicare & Medicaid Services (CMS)—an agency within the Department of Health and Human Services (HHS)—oversees Medicare, Medicaid, and CHIP. Medicare is the federal health insurance program for persons aged 65 or over, certain disabled individuals, and individuals with end-stage renal disease. Medicaid and CHIP are joint federal-state programs that finance health insurance coverage for certain categories of low-income adults and children.

[2]In fiscal year 2011, Medicare expenditures totaled approximately $565.6 billion; federal Medicaid expenditures were nearly $275 billion; and federal expenditures for CHIP were about $8.6 billion.

[3]Fraud involves an intentional act or representation to deceive with the knowledge that the action or representation could result in gain. The Health Care Fraud and Abuse Control Program received just over $608 million in fiscal year 2011. See *Department of Health and Human Services and Department of Justice, Health Care Fraud and Abuse Control Program Annual Report for Fiscal Year 2011*: February 2012. The program, which is under the joint direction of the Attorney General and the Secretary of HHS, is designed to coordinate federal, state, and local law enforcement activities with respect to health care fraud and abuse. Additional funds to combat health care fraud spent by HHS and the Department of Justice (DOJ) are not included in this figure.

GAO-12-820 Fraud in Medicare, Medicaid, and CHIP

and CHIP beneficiaries are subjects of fraud cases, including physicians, hospitals, durable medical equipment suppliers, home health agencies, and pharmacies.[4] Because their size and complexity make them vulnerable to fraud, we have designated Medicare and Medicaid as high-risk programs.[5] According to the Department of Health and Human Services' Office of Inspector General (HHS-OIG), common health care fraud schemes include providers or suppliers billing for services or supplies not provided or not medically necessary, purposely billing for a higher level of service than that provided, misreporting data to increase payments, paying kickbacks to providers for referring beneficiaries for specific services or to certain entities, and stealing providers' or beneficiaries' identities.

The Centers for Medicare & Medicaid Services (CMS)—an agency within the Department of Health and Human Services (HHS) that oversees Medicare, Medicaid, and CHIP—along with HHS-OIG, and the Department of Justice (DOJ)—including the Federal Bureau of Investigation (FBI)—work together to investigate and prosecute alleged fraud in Medicare, Medicaid, and CHIP. For example, CMS, HHS-OIG, and DOJ officials comprise Medicare Strike Force teams, which are designed to use data analysis techniques to identify and stop Medicare fraud. Additionally, these agencies coordinate with state Medicaid Fraud Control Units (MFCU), which are primarily responsible for investigating and prosecuting fraud within their state Medicaid programs.

HHS-OIG, FBI, and MFCUs receive referrals of alleged fraud from a variety of sources, including program beneficiaries, state agencies, law enforcement, and whistleblowers. CMS and its contractors report alleged fraud cases to HHS-OIG for investigation. HHS-OIG typically refers investigations of the alleged fraud cases that it believes have merit to DOJ for civil litigation or criminal prosecution because it does not have the authority to prosecute health care fraud cases. MFCUs—which are generally located in the state offices of the Attorney General—investigate and typically prosecute health care fraud cases under state laws. Additionally, MFCUs coordinate with HHS-OIG and DOJ on certain fraud

---

[4]Subjects of health care fraud cases can be individuals, such as a dentist or a nurse; an organization, such as a pharmaceutical manufacturer; or a facility, such as a hospital.

[5]See GAO, *High-Risk Series: An Update*, GAO-11-278 (Washington, D.C.: February 2011).

cases. DOJ and its divisions may also receive referrals of alleged fraud through civil cases filed by individuals under the False Claims Act (FCA). The outcomes of health care fraud cases can include civil and criminal penalties.[6] Civil penalties include monetary settlements, and criminal penalties include incarceration sentences, fines, and restitution. HHS-OIG also can impose administrative penalties on providers—including imposing a civil monetary penalty, or excluding a provider from participating in federal health care programs. In fiscal year 2011, the federal government won or negotiated approximately $2.4 billion in judgments and settlements related to health care fraud.[7]

Concerns have been raised about the need to better detect and combat fraud in federal health care programs, such as Medicare, Medicaid, and CHIP. Some of these concerns have specifically focused on determining whether resources to fight fraud are being targeted toward the types of health care providers committing the most fraud. This report provides information on individuals or entities involved in health care fraud cases in Medicare, Medicaid, and CHIP. These individuals and entities are generally referred to as "subjects" of health care fraud cases. In this report, we identify: (1) subjects of health care fraud cases by provider type involving Medicare, Medicaid, or CHIP that were handled by federal agencies, and changes in the types of providers in 2005 and 2010; and (2) subjects of health care fraud cases by provider type for those cases involving Medicaid or CHIP that were handled by MFCUs, and changes in the types of providers investigated in fraud cases in 2005 and 2010.

To identify subjects of health care fraud cases—including referrals, investigations, prosecutions, and outcomes—by provider type for cases involving Medicare, Medicaid, or CHIP that were handled by federal agencies, and to examine changes in the types of provider in 2005 and 2010, we obtained data on closed health care fraud cases from HHS-OIG, DOJ's Civil Division, and the Executive Office of U.S. Attorneys

---

[6]In this report, we use the term outcome to refer to the disposition of civil and criminal cases, which can include, among other things, convictions, monetary penalties, dismissals, and the decision not to pursue investigation or prosecution.

[7]We have previously reported that although there have been convictions for multimillion dollar schemes that defrauded the Medicare program, the extent of the problem is unknown. There are no reliable estimates of the extent of fraud in the Medicare program or for the health care industry as a whole. See GAO, *Medicare: Progress Made to Deter Fraud, but More Could Be Done*, GAO-12-801T (Washington, D.C.: June 8, 2012).

(EOUSA), which provides administrative support for the 94 U.S. Attorney's Offices (USAO).[8] We obtained data on fraud cases involving Medicare, Medicaid, and CHIP—including any cases that were closed in calendar years 2005 and 2010.[9] However, due to limitations with some of the 2005 data, our analysis of the changes in the types of providers in 2005 and 2010 is limited. Each fraud case can have more than one subject, and our analysis focuses on the subjects of the fraud cases rather than the cases themselves. Additionally, a fraud subject can be either an entity itself or an individual affiliated with an entity.[10] The data we received from HHS-OIG pertained only to health care fraud in Medicare, Medicaid, and CHIP; however, data we received from the USAOs and DOJ's Civil Division may also include other federal health care program fraud as well as fraud in the private sector as the databases used to track fraud cases do not capture fraud exclusively in Medicare, Medicaid, and CHIP. Since many fraud cases are handled jointly by HHS-OIG, USAOs, and DOJ's Civil Division (and entered into each agency's own database), we identified fraud case subjects that were in more than one data set we received by comparing subject information to the extent

---

[8]The USAOs are a division within DOJ that litigates both civil and criminal health care fraud cases in their districts throughout the country. Although the Federal Bureau of Investigation (FBI) investigates health care fraud and DOJ's Criminal Division prosecutes health care fraud, we did not obtain data from them because officials told us that the FBI and DOJ's Criminal Division primarily work on health care fraud cases jointly with the HHS-OIG or USAOs. Officials indicated that the vast majority of health care fraud cases handled by FBI and DOJ's Criminal Division would be entered in databases used either by HHS-OIG or USAOs. As a result, we did not request data from DOJ's Criminal Division or the FBI.

[9]We chose calendar year 2010 since HHS-OIG and DOJ and its divisions received additional funding for health care fraud activities in fiscal year 2010 and it was the most-recent complete year of data available at the time of our request. We chose calendar year 2005 to compare data we received for 2010 because this was before the Deficit Reduction Act was enacted, which increased funding for antifraud activities. We use the term "cases" throughout this report to refer to any suspected fraud information that was received by HHS-OIG, USAOs, or DOJ's Civil Division regardless of whether the case was formally investigated or prosecuted. Additionally, we refer to any cases received by HHS-OIG as investigations regardless of the level of resources expended on the case.

[10]For example, the subject of a fraud case could be a durable medical equipment supplier because the company billed for equipment that it did not provide, or could be an individual affiliated with the entity, such as an employee of a durable medical equipment supplier that billed for equipment not prescribed by a physician. In both of these examples, the entity involved is the durable medical equipment supplier, but in the first example the subject is the entity itself while in the second example the subject is an individual affiliated with the durable medical equipment supplier. In our analysis, we refer to subjects of fraud cases as the entities they are or the entities with which the individuals are affiliated.

possible. However, it is possible that our analysis still includes some duplication in fraud case subjects. With the exception of one analysis at the agency level, we excluded duplicate data so that each subject was only included once. The data we received from HHS-OIG contained information on the provider type of the subject; provider type is not a required field in the USAOs database, consequently, the USAOs do not consistently have provider type information, and DOJ's Civil Division does not collect data by provider type. In order to identify the provider type of subjects in the USAO and DOJ Civil Division data that were missing information, it was necessary for us to conduct an extensive search of publicly available court records to identify the provider type for 2,470 subjects. We searched for the subjects in the Public Access to Court Electronic Records (PACER) database and reviewed indictments, plea agreements, and other court documents to obtain information on the subject's provider type. After we identified the provider types for data we received from USAOs and DOJ's Civil Division and after reviewing the data on provider types in the HHS-OIG data, we aggregated the various provider types into broad categories, which are described in appendix I. We also reviewed agency documents and conducted interviews with officials from HHS-OIG and DOJ—including the Civil and Criminal Divisions, FBI, and EOUSA—to obtain information about health care fraud cases and the databases used to track these cases. To assess the reliability of the data, we interviewed officials from these agencies to discuss the quality of the data we obtained, reviewed relevant documentation, and examined the data for reasonableness and internal consistency. We found these data were sufficiently reliable for the purposes of our report (see app. I for additional information about our methodology).

To identify subjects of health care fraud cases by provider type for those cases involving Medicaid or CHIP that were handled by state MFCUs, and to examine changes in the types of providers investigated and prosecuted for fraud in 2005 and 2010, we collected aggregate data on closed fraud cases from 10 state MFCUs for 2005 and 2010. These MFCUs were selected because, collectively, they accounted for the majority of open fraud investigations, fraud indictments or charges, fraud convictions, amounts recovered from civil settlements and judgments, MFCU grant expenditures, and number of MFCU staff in fiscal year

2010.[11] The 10 selected MFCUs were in California, Florida, Illinois, Indiana, Louisiana, Massachusetts, New York, Ohio, Texas, and Virginia.[12] We developed a standardized data-collection instrument based on the HHS-OIG's Quarterly Statistical MFCU Report Template and accompanying definitions. We received feedback on a draft of the data-collection instrument from officials from two MFCUs before finalizing it. Although the data we received from the 10 MFCUs represent a majority of fraud cases handled by all MFCUs nationwide, the data are not generalizable to other states. The data we received represented actions related to fraud cases that occurred only in the years we requested.[13] Each instance of fraud in the data submitted by the 10 MFCUs represents one individual, facility, or organization that we refer to as the subject of the fraud case. Fraud case subjects may be an individual, such as a dentist or a nurse; an organization, such as a pharmaceutical manufacturer; or a facility, such as a hospital. Several subjects may be investigated in one fraud case; however, each subject in a fraud case is counted separately. Additionally, for our analysis, we aggregated various provider types into broad categories, which are described in appendix II. Because the state MFCUs may work together on certain cases that cross state lines, it is possible that duplicate data are included in our analysis. We also conducted interviews with officials from CMS, the HHS-OIG's Office of Evaluations and Inspections, and the National Association of MFCUs to obtain information on fraud cases handled by the MFCUs. We relied on the data as reported by the 10 MFCUs and did not independently verify these data. However, we reviewed the data for reasonableness and followed up with state officials for clarification when necessary. On the basis of these activities, we determined these data

---

[11]Nationwide, in fiscal year 2010 the selected state MFCUs accounted for 54.8 percent of open fraud investigations; 60.1 percent of fraud indictments and charges; 62.8 percent of fraud convictions; 40.6 percent of civil settlements and judgments; 66.0 percent of MFCU grant expenditures; and 64.1 percent of MFCU staff.

[12]We did not receive complete CHIP fraud data from Florida, New York, and Texas because the MFCUs in these states do not investigate fraud in CHIP. In the other seven states, data on CHIP fraud were included.

[13]We requested data from the state MFCUs for any actions—such as indictments, convictions, or penalties—that occurred on a subject's fraud case in 2005 or 2010. For example, if a subject was indicted in 2004 and sentenced in 2005, the MFCU data would only include information about the subject's sentencing in 2005, because the indictment occurred in a year outside of our data request.

were sufficiently reliable for the purpose of our report (see app. II for additional information).

We conducted this performance audit from June 2011 to September 2012 in accordance with generally accepted government auditing standards. Those standards require that we plan and perform the audit to obtain sufficient, appropriate evidence to provide a reasonable basis for our findings and conclusions based on our audit objectives. We believe that the evidence obtained provides a reasonable basis for any findings and conclusions based on our audit objectives.

Background

Medicare, Medicaid, and CHIP beneficiaries receive health care from a variety of providers and in different settings. When suspected cases of fraud emerge, many agencies are involved in investigating and prosecuting these cases and they rely on multiple statutes.

Medicare, Medicaid, and CHIP Health Care Providers

Medicare, Medicaid, and CHIP beneficiaries receive health care from a variety of providers—including physicians, nurses, dentists, and other medical professionals—in many different settings, such as hospitals, medical practices, clinics, and health centers. Additionally, beneficiaries may receive care and assistance from home health agencies and aides, durable medical equipment suppliers, and medical transportation companies. In 2010, about $478 billion in federal Medicare, Medicaid, and CHIP spending was attributable to hospital care (41.3 percent of total spending) and physician and clinical services (18.3 percent of total spending) based on National Health Expenditure Account data from CMS. Expenditures for prescription drugs accounted for 9.3 percent of spending in these programs, and nursing home care accounted for 7.8 percent. Many other categories of providers accounted for the remaining 23.4 percent.

Agencies That Investigate and Prosecute Health Care Fraud

Several agencies are involved in investigating and prosecuting health care fraud cases, including the HHS-OIG; DOJ's Civil and Criminal divisions; the 94 USAOs; the FBI; and state MFCUs. The HHS-OIG and FBI primarily conduct investigations of health care fraud, and DOJ's divisions typically prosecute or litigate those cases.[14] See table 1 for additional information about the role of each agency in fraud investigations and prosecutions.

Table 1: Agencies, Divisions, and Their Roles in Health Care Fraud Investigation and Prosecution

Agency	Division	Role in investigating and prosecuting health care fraud
Department of Health and Human Services' Office of Inspector General (HHS-OIG)	Office of Investigations	Responsible for conducting and coordinating investigations into allegations of fraud in HHS programs, including Medicare, Medicaid, and CHIP. They are also responsible for certain exclusions of providers from participating in federal health care programs.
		HHS-OIG investigators also play an active role in the Medicare Strike Force teams—which are teams comprising staff from federal, state, and local investigation agencies, designed to combat Medicare fraud by using data-analysis techniques—located in nine cities nationwide.
	Office of Counsel to the Inspector General	Has the authority to impose administrative penalties related to health care fraud, including civil monetary penalties.
Department of Justice (DOJ)[a]	Criminal Division	Prosecutes criminal health care fraud. DOJ's Criminal Division also plays an active role in the Medicare Strike Force teams.
	Civil Division	Represents the U.S. government in civil matters, such as cases brought against pharmaceutical manufacturers for marketing prescription drugs for uses other than what have been approved. DOJ's Civil Division also has the authority to bring criminal charges against pharmaceutical and medical device manufacturers for, among other things, unlawful off-label marketing under the Federal Food, Drug, and Cosmetic Act.
	U.S. Attorney's Offices (USAO)	Litigate or prosecute civil and criminal health care fraud cases in their districts—94 USAOs throughout the country. The USAOs in the nine cities where Medicare Strike Force teams are located also participate in those teams.
	Federal Bureau of Investigation (FBI)	Investigates health care fraud through coordinated initiatives with federal, state, and local agencies. The FBI also participates in task forces, and undercover operations to identify health care fraud, as well as the Medicare Strike Force teams.
Medicaid Fraud Control Unit (MFCU)	Each state and the District of Columbia has its own MFCU[b]	Investigate and typically prosecute civil and criminal health care fraud in the state's Medicaid program. The MFCUs also investigate cases of patient abuse and neglect. Although MFCUs typically work on Medicaid fraud cases, they may obtain permission from HHS-OIG to investigate fraud in Medicare.
		MFCUs are required to be separate and distinct from the state Medicaid agencies and receive state and federal Medicaid funds.

Source: GAO analysis of information from the HHS-OIG, DOJ and its divisions, and MFCUs.

[14]CMS and its contractors also conduct activities related to health care fraud. For example, CMS oversees the work of Zone Program Integrity Contractors, which are responsible for investigating potential fraud in Medicare fee-for-service in their assigned geographic area. These contractors identify suspect claims and provider billing patterns, investigate fraud leads, and refer suspected fraud cases to HHS-OIG.

GAO-12-820 Fraud in Medicare, Medicaid, and CHIP

These agencies often work together to investigate and prosecute health care fraud cases. For example, HHS-OIG may open a fraud case, work with the FBI during the investigation, and then refer the case to a USAO for prosecution. Additionally, HHS-OIG, the FBI, a USAO, and DOJ's Criminal Division work jointly on health care fraud cases handled by Medicare Strike Force teams. Health care fraud cases are opened by the agencies either when they receive information about suspected fraudulent activity from a source—which can include program beneficiaries and CMS and its contractors—or if they proactively identify possible fraudulent behavior through data analysis. Additionally, in civil cases known as qui tam cases, individuals—referred to as relators—with evidence of fraud can file a civil suit under the False Claims Act (FCA).[15] These qui tam cases are handled by a USAO or DOJ's Civil Division, though they may receive assistance in the investigation from HHS-OIG or the FBI. In other fraud cases, if a fraud case is opened by HHS-OIG, the agency typically conducts its investigation, determines whether the case has merit, and refers the case to DOJ for criminal prosecution or civil litigation. Alternatively, HHS-OIG may find that the case does not have merit and may close the case. HHS-OIG also has authority to impose civil monetary penalties or exclude the provider from participating in federal health care programs.[16] Similarly, DOJ's divisions may choose not to pursue a fraud case for a number of reasons, including a lack of evidence or insufficient

---

[15]The False Claims Act (FCA) prohibits certain actions, including the knowing presentation of a false claim for payment by the federal government. 31 U.S.C. § 3729(a)(1)(A). FCA claims may be brought by private persons—"relators" or "whistleblowers"—in the name of the government, alleging the submission of false claims. A qui tam case is a civil action brought by the relator for the person and for the government though the action is in the name of the government. In these qui tam cases, the relator can receive a portion of a monetary settlement, and reasonable expenses and attorneys' fees and costs. 31 U.S.C. § 3730(b),(d).

[16]Providers and individuals can be excluded for a variety of reasons other than for a health care fraud conviction, including licensure suspension, surrender, or revocation, patient abuse/neglect conviction, or felony controlled substance conviction. Under section 1128 of the Social Security Act, exclusions from federal health programs are mandatory under certain circumstances and permissive in others. 42 U.S.C. § 1320a-7.

evidence to support the charges, or a lack of resources for investigation or prosecution.[17]

MFCUs investigate and typically prosecute health care fraud cases in the state's Medicaid program under state laws, and frequently coordinate with HHS-OIG and DOJ on the investigation and prosecution of certain fraud cases. Many MFCUs have authority to prosecute cases of fraud, but not all MFCUs are able to do so and refer cases to other agencies for prosecution. For example, Texas' MFCU does not have the authority to prosecute cases and refers cases to another agency or office, such as the U.S. Attorney's Office or the state's District Attorney, for prosecution.

Fraud Statutes and Outcomes

Several statutes concern health care fraud.[18] These statutes include the following:

- Civil monetary penalty provisions of the Social Security Act are applicable to certain enumerated activities, such as knowingly presenting a claim for medical services that is known to be false and fraudulent.[19] The Social Security Act also provides for criminal penalties for knowing and willful false statements in applications for payment.[20] In addition, providers may be excluded on a mandatory or permissive basis from participating in federal health care programs for engaging in certain fraudulent activities.

- The Anti-Kickback statute makes it a criminal offense for anyone to knowingly and willfully solicit, receive, offer, or pay any remuneration in return for or to induce referrals of items or services reimbursable under a federal health care program, subject to statutory exceptions and regulatory safe harbors.[21] For example, a payment program

---

[17]DOJ has to review and decide whether to intervene in qui tam cases within a statutorily specified amount of time.

[18]The statutes included here provide examples of those that may be relevant to health care fraud cases. Other statutory provisions, including those located in title 18 of the United States Code, may also be relevant to such cases. *See, e.g.,* 18 U.S.C. §§ 669 (concerning theft or embezzlement in connection with health care), 1035 (concerning false statements relating to health care matters), and 1347 (concerning health care fraud).

[19]42 U.S.C. § 1320a-7a.

[20]42 U.S.C. § 1320a-7b.

[21]42 U.S.C. § 1320a-7b(b).

GAO-12-820 Fraud in Medicare, Medicaid, and CHIP

under which a hospital paid physicians who referred patients for admission would implicate the anti-kickback statute.

- The Stark law and its implementing regulations prohibit physicians from making "self-referrals"—certain referrals for "designated health services" paid for by Medicare[22] to entities with which the physician (or immediate family) has a financial relationship. The Stark law also prohibits these entities that perform the "designated health services" from presenting claims to Medicare or billing for these services.[23]

- The Federal Food, Drug, and Cosmetic Act makes it unlawful to, among other things, introduce an adulterated or misbranded pharmaceutical product or device into interstate commerce.[24]

- The False Claims Act (FCA) is often used by the federal government in health care fraud cases.[25] The FCA prohibits certain actions, including the knowing presentation of a false claim for payment by the federal government. Claims that are submitted in violation of certain other statutes may also be considered false claims and, as a result, create additional liability under the FCA. Many health care fraud cases pursued under the FCA are for billing for goods or services not rendered, billing for unnecessary health care goods or services, or billing for goods or services at a higher rate than what was provided. Under the FCA, civil cases can be brought by the U.S. government or by a private citizen.

The outcome of a fraud case can depend on whether the case is civil or criminal, and if the case is prosecuted or litigated, the penalties authorized under the relevant statutes. For example, civil cases that are litigated may result in judgments imposed by a court or settlements reached by the subjects and litigators of the fraud case. In criminal cases, outcomes can include incarceration, probation, and fines. HHS-OIG may also impose civil monetary penalties on providers for committing fraud, and may exclude providers from participating in federal health care

---

[22]The Social Security Act prohibits payments to states for Medicaid services that would be prohibited by Medicare under the Stark law. 42 U.S.C. § 1396b(s).

[23]42 U.S.C. § 1395nn(a)(1).

[24]21 U.S.C. § 331(a).

[25]31 U.S.C. §§ 3729-3733.

programs. In some cases, a subject may receive both civil and criminal penalties, and be excluded.

Medical Facilities Were the Most Frequent Subjects of Criminal Investigations, and Hospitals Were the Most Frequent Subjects of Civil Investigations

According to 2010 data, 10,187 subjects were investigated for health care fraud. Medical facilities (such as medical centers, clinics, and medical practices) and durable medical equipment suppliers were the most frequent subjects of criminal fraud cases in 2010. Hospitals and medical facilities were the most frequent subjects of civil fraud cases, including cases that resulted in judgments or settlements. Nearly 2,200 individuals were excluded from program participation by HHS-OIG, about 60 percent of whom were in the nursing profession.

Approximately 10,200 Subjects Were Investigated for Health Care Fraud in 2010

According to 2010 data, 10,187 subjects were investigated for health care fraud—of which, 7,848 were subjects of criminal fraud cases, and 2,339 were subjects of civil fraud cases. Data from 2010 shows that HHS-OIG investigated health care fraud cases for nearly 8,900 subjects, many more than were opened by the USAOs and DOJ's Civil Division.[26] Table 2 contains information on health care fraud subjects by agency, reflecting the work of each agency in 2010. To fully reflect the work of each agency, data on subjects that were included in more than one agency database were included in the top portion of the table. The duplicate cases were removed to arrive at the unique count of subjects and were not included in our other analyses. Data comparing cases handled in 2005 and 2010 show that HHS-OIG investigated cases for nearly 2,800 more subjects in 2010 than it did in 2005, while the USAOs and DOJ's Civil Division handled cases for approximately the same number of subjects.

---

[26]As previously mentioned, each fraud case can have more than one subject involved. According to 2010 data, there were 4,709 criminal cases and 1,024 civil cases.

Table 2: Number of Subjects Investigated in Health Care Fraud Cases, by Agency, 2010

Agency	Subjects of criminal cases	Subjects of civil cases	Total
HHS-OIG	7,270	1,606	**8,876**
USAOs	877	545	**1,422**
DOJ's Civil Division	n/a	445	**445**
Subjects that were included in more than one agency database[a]	(299)	(257)	**(556)**
Unique count of subjects investigated in fraud cases	**7,848**	**2,339**	**10,187**

Source: GAO analysis of Department of Health and Human Services' Office of Inspector General (HHS-OIG), Department of Justice's (DOJ) U.S. Attorneys' Offices (USAO), and DOJ's Civil Division data.

Notes: Data in this table are for calendar year 2010. The data from HHS-OIG pertained only to health care fraud in Medicare, Medicaid, and the Children's Health Insurance Program (CHIP); however, data from the USAOs and DOJ's Civil Division may also include other health care fraud.

DOJ's Civil Division handles civil health care fraud cases and has the authority to bring criminal charges against pharmaceutical and medical device manufacturers under the Federal Food, Drug, and Cosmetic Act.

[a]Health care fraud data reported in this table contain duplicate information for some subjects of the fraud cases because fraud cases are often jointly handled by HHS-OIG, USAOs, and DOJ's Civil Division, and information about these cases are entered into each agency's own database. We excluded duplicate information for subjects that we identified in more than one agency database so that each subject was only included once in our analysis.

According to 2010 HHS-OIG data, most of the subjects involved in fraud cases were referred to HHS-OIG by federal law enforcement agencies—such as the FBI—(38 percent), or state or local law enforcement agencies (10 percent).[27] Case subjects were also referred to HHS-OIG by CMS contractors tasked with program integrity (14 percent), current or former employees of providers (9 percent), or individuals (9 percent), and the remainder were from other sources. (See table 3 for additional information on the source of health care fraud cases referred to HHS-OIG.)

---

[27]The data we received from the USAOs and DOJ's Civil Division did not contain information on the source of the fraud case. However, officials from DOJ indicated that they generally receive fraud cases from HHS-OIG, the FBI, or from relators who have filed claims under the False Claims Act.

GAO-12-820 Fraud in Medicare, Medicaid, and CHIP

Table 3: Number and Percentage of Subjects of Health Care Fraud Cases Referred to HHS-OIG, by Source of Referral, 2010

	Criminal	Civil	Total	Percentage of total
Federal law enforcement	3,022	337	**3,359**	37.8%
CMS program integrity contractors	1,113	122	**1,235**	13.9
State, local, or tribal law enforcement agency	805	62	**867**	9.8
Current or former employees of providers	783	53	**836**	9.4
Individuals who are unaffiliated	778	44	**822**	9.3
Qui Tam[a]	71	684	**755**	8.5
Other	486	128	**614**	6.9
State, local, or tribal non-law-enforcement agency	203	54	**257**	2.9
Self-disclosure[b]	9	122	**131**	1.5
Total	**7,270**	**1,606**	**8,876**	**100%**

Source: GAO analysis of Department of Health and Human Services' Office of Inspector General (HHS-OIG) data.

Notes: The data included in this table represent information about the source of the fraud case, which can include more than one subject and are for calendar year 2010. The data from HHS-OIG pertained only to health care fraud in Medicare, Medicaid, and the Children's Health Insurance Program (CHIP).

[a]Qui tam cases are brought under the False Claims Act by a private citizen.

[b]Self-disclosure refers to cases where providers report any improper actions to HHS-OIG themselves.

Medical Facilities and Durable Medical Equipment Suppliers Were the Most Frequent Subjects of Criminal Fraud Cases in 2010

About 49 percent of criminal health care fraud subjects were, or were affiliated with, medical facilities (such as medical practices, clinics, or centers), durable medical equipment suppliers, and home health agencies. Of the 7,848 subjects associated with criminal cases, about 1,100 were charged, and 85 percent of those charged were found guilty or pled guilty or no contest. Of those subjects who were found guilty or pled guilty or no contest, about 37 percent were medical facilities and durable medical equipment suppliers.

Criminal Health Care Fraud

Example of a Criminal Health Care Fraud Investigation

According to the indictment in one fraud case, two subjects owned and operated a medical clinic that provided injection treatments for patients with cancer, HIV, or AIDS. The owners paid cash kickbacks and bribes to Medicare beneficiaries to serve as patients at the medical clinic, and submitted claims to the Medicare program for services that were not provided, not provided as claimed, or were not medically necessary. To make it appear that they operated a legitimate clinic, one of the owners ordered quantities of specific HIV and AIDS medications, but the quantity of drugs ordered was much less than the quantity billed to Medicare. Medicare made payments of nearly $2.1 million to the clinic.

According to 2010 data, many different types of providers—including medical facilities and hospitals, or individuals affiliated with these entities—were suspected of health care fraud.[28] Specifically, about one-quarter of subjects investigated in criminal health care fraud cases were medical facilities or were affiliated with these facilities. Additionally, about 16 percent of subjects were durable medical equipment suppliers. Over 19 percent were subjects for which we could not determine an affiliation. See table 4 for additional information on the subjects of criminal health care fraud cases by provider type for 2010.

---

[28]Subjects of the fraud cases could be the entities themselves, such as a durable medical equipment supplier that billed for equipment that it did not provide, or individuals affiliated with an entity, such as an employee of a durable medical equipment supplier that billed for equipment not prescribed by a physician. In both of these cases, the entity involved is the durable medical equipment supplier, but in the first example the subject is the entity itself while in the second example the subject is an individual affiliated with the durable medical equipment supplier. We generally refer to the subjects of fraud cases as the entities with which they are affiliated.

Table 4: Number and Percentage of Subjects in Criminal Health Care Fraud Investigations, by Provider Type, 2010

	Number of subjects of criminal cases	Percentage of total criminal cases
Medical facilities		
Medical practices	1,101	24.3%
Medical centers or clinics	807	
Durable medical equipment suppliers	1,275	16.2
Home health agencies	639	8.1
Other centers, clinics, or facilities	598	7.6
Hospitals	357	4.5
Pharmacies	321	4.1
Nursing homes	253	3.2
Management service providers	209	2.7
Medical transportation companies	200	2.5
Other	162	2.1
Mental health centers or clinics	122	1.6
Government employees, contractors, or grantees	103	1.3
Insurance companies	79	1.0
Dental clinics or practices	55	0.7
Pharmaceutical manufacturers or suppliers	38	0.5
Medical supply companies	18	0.2
Unknown affiliation		
Health care providers	779	
Individuals[a]	668	19.2
Data unavailable	64	
Total	**7,848**	

Source: GAO analysis of Department of Health and Human Services' Office of Inspector General (HHS-OIG) and Department of Justice's (DOJ) U.S. Attorneys' Offices (USAO) data.

Notes: Data in this table are for calendar year 2010. The data from HHS-OIG pertained only to health care fraud in Medicare, Medicaid, and the Children's Health Insurance Program (CHIP); however, data from the USAOs may also include other health care fraud.

Each unique subject is only counted once in this table. We identified 299 subjects of criminal cases that were duplicate subjects in the 2010 data. We removed these duplicate subjects from the analysis reported here.

For the subjects in the DOJ's USAO data, we identified the provider type using the court documents obtained from the Public Access to Court Electronic Records (PACER) database.

[a]Individuals whose affiliation was unknown include some who were not health care providers. For example, this category includes individuals who were investigated for health care fraud because they obtained illegal prescription drugs from physicians or pharmacies.

GAO-12-820 Fraud in Medicare, Medicaid, and CHIP

Among the 7,848 subjects in 2010 criminal cases, nearly 50 percent were the entities themselves, rather than individuals affiliated with those entities. See table 5 for more detailed information on the types of providers that were subjects in 2010 criminal cases. Of the 3,864 subjects that were entities, most were durable medical equipment suppliers (819), home health agencies (507), medical centers or clinics (506), or medical practices (486). Additionally, more than 15 percent were physicians, and about 14 percent were management employees—such as owners, operators, or managers.

Table 5: Number and Percentage of Subjects in Criminal Health Care Fraud Investigations, by Entity or Individual Provider Type, 2010

	Number of subjects of criminal cases	Percentage of total criminal cases
Entities		
Durable medical equipment suppliers	819	
Home health agencies	507	
Medical centers or clinics	506	
Medical practices	486	
Hospitals	336	49.2%
Other centers, clinics, or facilities	330	
Nursing homes	202	
Pharmacies	196	
Other entities	482	
Entities subtotal	**3,864**	
Individuals		
Physicians	1,208	15.4
Management employees		
Durable medical equipment suppliers	420	
Medical centers or clinics	185	13.6
Home health agencies	85	
Other entities	375	
Employees	517	6.6
Individuals that were not affiliated with an entity and were not health care providers	344	4.4
Recipients and beneficiaries	258	3.3
Nurses, nurses' aides, or health care aides	166	2.1
Other[a]	426	5.4
Individuals subtotal	**3,984**	
Total	**7,848**	

Source: GAO analysis of Department of Health and Human Services' Office of Inspector General (HHS-OIG) and Department of Justice's (DOJ) U.S. Attorneys' Offices (USAO) data.

Notes: Data in this table are for calendar year 2010. For the subjects in the Department of Justice's U.S. Attorneys' Offices data, we identified the provider type using the court documents obtained from the Public Access to Court Electronic Records (PACER) database. The data from HHS-OIG pertained only to health care fraud in Medicare, Medicaid, and the Children's Health Insurance Program (CHIP); however, data from the USAOs may have also included other health care fraud.

[a]This category includes pharmacists, psychologists, therapists, counselors, physician assistants, dentists, and other individuals.

Changes in Provider Types in 2005 and 2010

Our data show that 2010 criminal cases involved 2,300 more subjects than 2005 cases. Additionally, some provider types had particularly large increases in 2010 compared to the number of subjects investigated in criminal cases in 2005. For example, cases where pharmacies were the subjects increased from 99 subjects in 2005 to 321 in 2010 (an increase of 224 percent), and the number of home health agency subjects increased from 284 to 639 (an increase of 125 percent). The 2005 data show that medical facilities and durable medical equipment suppliers were the provider types with the most subjects investigated in cases, as was also the case with 2010 data. In 2005, medical facilities represented 23 percent of all subjects in criminal cases, and durable medical equipment suppliers accounted for 18 percent. Similarly, in 2010, medical facilities accounted for 24 percent of all subjects in criminal cases, and durable medical equipment suppliers accounted for 16 percent.

Outcomes for the Subjects of Criminal Fraud Cases from 2010 Data

Most of the 7,848 subjects who were investigated for criminal fraud in 2010 were not pursued—meaning that HHS-OIG did not refer the subject's case to DOJ for prosecution. Most subjects—about 85 percent—were investigated in criminal cases that were not pursued for a variety of reasons, mainly due to lack of resources or insufficient evidence. The 2010 data indicated that 1,086 subjects were charged in criminal fraud cases, which represented about 14 percent of all criminal case subjects. Additionally, nearly 1 percent of subjects were involved in criminal case appeals, most of which were decided favorably for the U.S. government. See table 6 for additional information about the number of subjects in criminal cases by outcome.

Table 6: Number and Percentage of Subjects Investigated in Criminal Health Care Fraud Cases, by Outcome of Case, 2010

	Number of subjects	Number of subjects by category	Percentage of total subjects by category
Subjects that were charged[a]			
Found guilty or pled guilty or no contest	925		
Acquitted	13	1,086	14%
Subject's case was dismissed	102		
Other outcome, such as pretrial diversion	46		
Subjects whose cases were not pursued[b]			
Lack of resources	2,219		
Lack of sufficient evidence or insufficient details	904		
Subject's case did not meet guidance, was outside of HHS-OIG jurisdiction, or violation occurred outside of HHS-OIG's region	338	6,700	85
Subject already under investigation or investigated in another case	336		
Other reasons[c]	2,903		
Subjects who appealed their original cases			
Appeal was dismissed by appellant	5		
Appeal decision was favorable for the U.S. government	55	62	1
Appeal decision was not favorable for the U.S. government	2		
Total	**7,848**		

Source: GAO analysis of data obtained from Department of Health and Human Services' Office of Inspector General (HHS-OIG) and Department of Justice's (DOJ) U.S. Attorneys' Office (USAO).

Notes: Data in this table are for calendar year 2010. The data from HHS-OIG pertained only to health care fraud in Medicare, Medicaid, and the Children's Health Insurance Program (CHIP); however, data from the USAOs may have also included other health care fraud.

[a]Subjects in this section were involved in cases that were pursued, meaning that the USAOs received the case and took some sort of action on it. For example, in some cases, the USAO received the case and decided to dismiss the charges while in others the USAO prosecuted the case and the subject was found guilty.

[b]Subjects in this section were from cases that were not pursued further than the case being received or investigated by HHS-OIG. For these cases, HHS-OIG did not refer them to the USAOs for prosecution for the reasons included in this section of the table.

[c]Other reasons include that the allegations in the case did not constitute a violation or the criminal case was closed to pursue a civil case, impose a civil monetary penalty, or exclude the provider. Some subjects had their cases closed by HHS-OIG rather than referring the case to the USAOs for prosecution for undetermined reasons.

Among the 1,086 subjects that were charged, over 85 percent (925 subjects) were found guilty, pled guilty, or pled no contest to some or all of the criminal charges against them. For the remaining 15 percent of subjects, charges were dismissed (9.4 percent), subjects were found not guilty (1.2 percent), or had another outcome (4.2 percent).[29]

Of the 925 subjects who were found guilty or pled guilty or no contest, about 19 percent were from medical facilities—including medical centers, clinics, or practices. Although 2010 Medicare, Medicaid, and CHIP expenditures on durable medical equipment services was 1.3 percent of total spending in those programs, approximately 19 percent of subjects that were found guilty or pled guilty or no contest were durable medical equipment suppliers. Many different provider types were among the remaining subjects found guilty or that pled guilty or no contest. We could not identify the affiliation of nearly one-third of the subjects, including both health care providers and individuals. See table 7 for additional information on these subjects in 2010 criminal cases by provider type.

---

[29]Subjects involved in cases where there was another outcome included subjects that had pretrial diversions, were charged in other cases, or were involved in cases that were transferred to another district.

Table 7: Number and Percentage of Health Care Fraud Subjects That Were Found Guilty or Pled Guilty or No Contest, by Provider Type, 2010

	Number of subjects that were found guilty or pled guilty or no contest	Percentage of total number of subjects that were found guilty or pled guilty or no contest
Medical facilities		
Medical centers or clinics	130	18.7%
Medical practices	43	
Durable medical equipment suppliers	171	18.5
Other centers, clinics, or facilities	58	6.3
Other	49	5.3
Home health agencies	42	4.5
Pharmacies	40	4.3
Management service providers	33	3.6
Nursing homes	14	1.5
Medical transportation companies	14	1.5
Pharmaceutical manufacturers or suppliers	9	1.0
Mental health centers, clinics, or facilities	9	1.0
Medical supply companies	8	0.9
Insurance companies	5	0.5
Dental clinics or practices	4	0.4
Government employees, contractors, or grantees	3	0.3
Hospitals	2	0.2
Unknown affiliation		
Individuals	220	31.6
Health care providers	52	
Data unavailable	19	
Total	**925**	

Source: GAO analysis of Department of Health and Human Services' Office of Inspector General (HHS-OIG) and Department of Justice's (DOJ) U.S. Attorneys' Offices (USAO).

Notes: Data in this table are for calendar year 2010. For the subjects in the DOJ's USAO data, we identified the provider type using the court documents obtained from the Public Access to Court Electronic Records database. The data from HHS-OIG pertained only to health care fraud in Medicare, Medicaid, and the Children's Health Insurance Program; however, data from the USAOs may have also included other health care fraud.

GAO-12-820 Fraud in Medicare, Medicaid, and CHIP

Of the 925 subjects who were found guilty or pled guilty or no contest, 60 percent were sentenced to incarceration,[30] and 73 percent were sentenced to probation. Nearly 26 percent of those sentenced to incarceration were subjects affiliated with durable medical equipment suppliers, and 21 percent were affiliated with medical facilities. Similarly, both durable medical equipment suppliers and medical facilities each represented 17 percent of subjects sentenced to probation. The average length of a sentence to incarceration was about 3.5 years, and the maximum sentence received was a life sentence. Nearly 60 percent of subjects sentenced to incarceration received sentences between 2 and 5 years, while nearly 21 percent received a term of 1 year or less. More than 13 percent received sentences between 6 and 10 years and about 5 percent received sentences of more than 10 years of incarceration. The average probation term was 2.8 years, and the maximum term was 10 years. Nearly 78 percent of subjects sentenced to probation received a probation term between 2 and 5 years.

Subjects of criminal fraud cases could also be sentenced to home detention, public service, or their sentences could be suspended. Additionally, subjects could also be ordered to pay fines and restitution. Data from HHS-OIG contained information on these types of penalties, but data we received from the USAOs did not. According to 2010 data from HHS-OIG

- 56 subjects were sentenced to home detention terms;

- 75 subjects were sentenced to complete public service;

- 31 subjects received suspended sentences;

- 440 subjects were required to pay a fine; and

- 307 subjects were required to pay restitution.

---

[30]An official at HHS-OIG told us that it captures information on whether the subjects were sentenced to be incarcerated but does not capture information on whether the subjects were sentenced to serve that term in jail or prison, and a USAO official indicated that subjects sentenced to incarceration serve those sentences in prison.

GAO-12-820 Fraud in Medicare, Medicaid, and CHIP

Among those subjects that were required to pay fines or restitution, or both, the average amounts required were $898,361 in fines, and $1.8 million in restitution. In total, subjects were ordered to pay nearly $960 million in combined fines and restitution.[31]

Hospitals and Medical Facilities Were the Most Frequent Subjects of Civil Fraud Cases, Including Cases That Resulted in Judgments or Settlements

According to 2010 civil case data for health care fraud, 2,339 subjects were investigated in civil cases. Hospitals represented nearly 20 percent of these subjects, and medical facilities about 18 percent. Civil cases involving approximately 1,100 subjects were pursued—meaning that the USAOs or DOJ's Civil Division received the cases and took some sort of action, such as litigating the case; and of those, 55 percent resulted in a judgment for the government or in a settlement. For those cases that resulted in a judgment or settlement, or both, about 44 percent of the subjects were hospitals and medical facilities.

Civil Health Care Fraud

According to 2010 data, hospitals were nearly 20 percent of the subjects of civil fraud cases, and medical facilities were also frequently the subjects of civil cases, making up about 18 percent of the subjects. We were unable to determine the provider type or their affiliation for about 18 percent of the subjects of civil cases. (See table 8 for additional information on the subjects of civil health care fraud cases by provider type for 2010.)

Example of a Civil Health Care Fraud Investigation

According to the court document for a qui tam case, a nurse employed at a rehabilitation hospital alleged that a physician defrauded Medicare by upcoding hospital visits to more expensive procedures and billed Medicare for work on days he did not work. In addition, the physician and the hospital conspired to defraud Medicare by admitting patients who did not qualify for inpatient treatment and keeping patients in the hospital who were not benefiting from inpatient hospitalization. The hospital assigned a disproportionate share of admitted patients to the physician engaged in fraud.

---

[31]According to 2010 data from HHS-OIG, subjects of criminal cases were ordered to pay about $395 million in fines and $565 million in restitution. Although the subjects were ordered to pay these amounts, the amounts actually recovered from them may be less than what was ordered. HHS-OIG also receives recoveries, which is money returned administratively—such as through self-disclosure, demand letters, or prepayment prior to disposition—rather than settlements or judgments.

Table 8: Number and Percentage of Civil Health Care Fraud Case Subjects Investigated, by Provider Type, 2010

	Number of subjects of civil cases	Percentage of total civil cases
Hospitals	455	19.5%
Medical facilities		
Medical practices	218	17.7
Medical centers or clinics	197	
Other centers, clinics, or facilities	145	6.2
Home health agencies	120	5.1
Pharmaceutical manufacturers or suppliers	108	4.6
Durable medical equipment suppliers	102	4.4
Management service providers	101	4.3
Nursing homes	100	4.3
Pharmacies	75	3.2
Insurance companies	74	3.2
Other	55	2.4
Mental health centers, clinics, or facilities	42	1.8
Government employees, contractors, or grantees	32	1.4
Dental clinics or practices	31	1.3
Medical transportation companies	29	1.2
Medical supply companies	25	1.1
Unknown affiliation		
Data unavailable or incomplete	218	
Health care providers	190	18.3
Individuals	22	
Total	**2,339**	

Source: GAO analysis of Department of Health and Human Services' Office of Inspector General (HHS-OIG), Department of Justice's (DOJ) U.S. Attorneys' Offices (USAO), and DOJ's Civil Division data.

Notes: Data in this table are for calendar year 2010. The data from HHS-OIG pertained only to health care fraud in Medicare, Medicaid, and the Children's Health Insurance Program (CHIP); however, data from the USAOs and DOJ's Civil Division may have also included other health care fraud.

Fraud cases are often jointly handled by HHS-OIG, USAOs, and DOJ's Civil Division. As a result, the data we received contain duplicate information for some of the subjects of fraud cases. We identified 257 subjects of civil cases that were duplicate subjects in the 2010 data and removed these duplicate subjects from the analysis reported here.

For the subjects in the USAOs and DOJ's Civil Division data, we identified the provider type using the court documents obtained from the Public Access to Court Electronic Records (PACER) database.

GAO-12-820 Fraud in Medicare, Medicaid, and CHIP

As previously mentioned, individuals can bring civil health care fraud suits, known as qui tam cases, under the FCA. According to 2010 data from the USAOs and DOJ's Civil Division, 88 percent of subjects investigated in civil cases were investigated in qui tam cases.

Nearly 61 percent of the subjects investigated in 2010 civil cases were entities themselves, rather than individuals affiliated with those entities. Most of these entities were hospitals, medical centers or clinics, medical practices, or pharmaceutical manufacturers or suppliers. Additionally, physicians represented 12 percent of the subjects; and management employees, such as owners, operators, or managers, represented 8 percent of the civil case subjects. (See table 9 for more-detailed information on the types of providers that were subjects in 2010 civil cases.)

Table 9: Number and Percentage of Civil Health Care Fraud Case Subjects Investigated, by Entity or Individual Provider Type, 2010

	Number of subjects of civil cases	Percentage of total civil cases
Entities		
Hospitals	432	
Medical centers or clinics	121	
Medical practices	121	
Pharmaceutical manufacturers or suppliers	108	
Home health agencies	91	60.6%
Nursing homes	83	
Durable medical equipment suppliers	82	
Management service providers	82	
Other entities	298	
Entities subtotal	**1,418**	
Individuals		
Physicians	284	12.1
Management employees	194	8.3
Employees	94	4.0
Nurses, nurses' aides, or health care aides	29	1.2
Other[a]	320	13.7
Individuals subtotal	**921**	
Total	**2,339**	

Source: GAO analysis of Department of Health and Human Services' Office of Inspector General (HHS-OIG), Department of Justice's (DOJ) U.S. Attorneys' Offices (USAO), and DOJ's Civil Division data.

Notes: Data in this table are for calendar year 2010. For the subjects in the USAOs and DOJ's Civil Division data, we identified the provider type using the court documents obtained from the Public Access to Court Electronic Records (PACER) database. The data from HHS-OIG pertained only to health care fraud in Medicare, Medicaid, and the Children's Health Insurance Program (CHIP); however, data from the USAOs and DOJ's Civil Division may have also included other health care fraud.

[a]This category includes pharmacists, psychologists, therapists, counselors, physician assistants, dentists, recipients and beneficiaries, and others.

Civil Case Subjects in 2005 and 2010

In 2010, over 600 more subjects were investigated in civil cases than in 2005, about a 35 percent total increase. Changes in provider types for civil cases are not reported here because we were unable to identify provider types for about 31 percent of the subjects in the 2005 data. In the 2010 data, we were unable to identify the provider type for about 18 percent of subjects. Because of this limitation, the percentage increases in certain provider types investigated in civil fraud cases may

GAO-12-820 Fraud in Medicare, Medicaid, and CHIP

not be an accurate reflection of the actual increases in provider types of civil fraud cases.

Outcomes for Subjects of Civil Fraud Cases in 2010

Not all of the subjects investigated in 2010 civil cases were pursued—meaning that the USAOs or DOJ's Civil Division received the case and took some sort of action. According to the data we received, 1,087 subjects were involved in civil cases that were pursued, representing nearly 47 percent of all civil case subjects. Among other subjects of civil cases, more than 53 percent were not pursued for numerous reasons, including a lack of resources or insufficient evidence. Additionally, less than 1 percent of subjects were involved in civil appeals cases. (See table 10 for additional information about the number of subjects involved in civil cases by outcome.)

Table 10: Number and Percentage of Subjects in Civil Health Care Fraud Cases, by Outcome of Case, 2010

	Number of subjects	Number of subjects by category	Percentage of total subjects by category
Subjects in civil case investigations that were pursued[a]			
Judgment for U.S. government or relator, or settlement, or both	602		
Judgment for opposition (subject)	11		
Case was declined	33		
Case was voluntarily dismissed[b]	315	1,087	46.5%
Case was closed with necessary actions taken	70		
Other outcome	56		
Subjects in civil case investigations that were not pursued[c]			
Lack of resources	271		
Lack of sufficient evidence or insufficient details	58		
Subject already under investigation or investigated in another case	66	1,246	53.3
Other reasons[d]	851		
Subjects who appealed their original cases			
Appeal was dismissed by appellant	2		
Appeal decision was favorable for the U.S.	4	6	0.3
Total	**2,339**		

Source: GAO analysis of data obtained from Department of Health and Human Services' Office of Inspector General (HHS-OIG), Department of Justice's (DOJ) U.S. Attorneys' Office (USAO) and DOJ's Civil Division data.

Notes: Data in this table are for calendar year 2010. The data from HHS-OIG pertained only to health care fraud in Medicare, Medicaid, and the Children's Health Insurance Program (CHIP); however, data from the USAOs and DOJ's Civil Division may have also included other health care fraud.

[a]Subjects in this section were involved in cases that were pursued, meaning that the USAOs or DOJ's Civil Division received the case and took some sort of action on it. For example, in some cases, DOJ's Civil Division received the case and declined to intervene while in others DOJ's Civil Division litigated the case and the court issued a judgment against the subject.

Example of a Civil Health Care Fraud Case Judgment

In one civil case judgment that was pursued under the False Claims Act, a medical clinic was accused of billing Medicare for infusion therapy treatments allegedly provided by a physician; however, the physician indicated that he did not provide those treatments and several beneficiaries complained that claims were submitted for services never provided to them. The fraudulent claims were submitted for a drug that was not approved for use in patients with the conditions listed on the claims. This case was pursued in court and resulted in a judgment for the U.S. government of more than $17 million.

According to data from the USAOs and DOJ's Civil Division, most qui tam cases did not result in a judgment or settlement. For example, 52 percent of subjects in qui tam cases were either voluntarily dismissed by the relator (34 percent) or were declined by the USAOs or DOJ's Civil Division (18 percent). Nearly 24 percent of qui tam cases were settled and in 8 percent of qui tam cases there was a judgment for the government.[32]

For the 602 subjects for which cases resulted in a settlement or judgment for the government or for the relator, 27 percent of the subjects were hospitals and about 17 percent were medical facilities. For nearly 16 percent of subjects, we were unable to determine the affiliation of the provider or individual. (See table 11 for information on provider types for subjects where the case resulted in a settlement or judgment for the government or relator.)

---

[32]Nearly 15 percent of subjects were involved in cases where the case had another outcome, such as the case was transferred from the district or the court dismissed the case on a motion. Additionally, 1.6 percent of subjects were involved in qui tam cases where there was a judgment for the opposing party.

Table 11: Number and Percentage of Subjects in Civil Health Care Fraud Cases with Judgment for Government or Relator, or Settlement, or Both, by Provider Type, 2010

	Number of subjects with judgment or settlement, or both	Percentage of total number of subjects with judgment or settlement, or both
Hospitals	165	27.4%
Medical facilities		
Medical practices	65	16.6
Medical centers or clinics	35	
Other centers, clinics, or facilities	41	6.8
Home health agencies	34	5.6
Nursing homes	26	4.3
Durable medical equipment suppliers	25	4.2
Management service providers	21	3.5
Dental clinics or practices	21	3.5
Pharmaceutical manufacturers or suppliers	19	3.2
Insurance companies	15	2.5
Pharmacies	13	2.2
Medical transportation companies	11	1.8
Mental health centers, clinics, or facilities	5	0.8
Other	5	0.8
Medical supply companies	3	0.5
Government employees, contractors, or grantees	2	0.3
Unknown affiliation		
Data unavailable	58	15.9
Health care providers	34	
Individuals	4	
Total	**602**	

Source: GAO analysis of Department of Health and Human Services' Office of Inspector General (HHS-OIG), Department of Justice's (DOJ) U.S. Attorneys' Offices (USAO), and DOJ's Civil Division data.

Notes: Data in this table are for calendar year 2010. For the subjects in the USAOs and DOJ's Civil Division data, we identified the provider type using the court documents obtained from the Public Access to Court Electronic Records (PACER) database. The data from HHS-OIG pertained only to health care fraud in Medicare, Medicaid, and the Children's Health Insurance Program (CHIP); however, data from the USAOs and DOJ's Civil Division may have also included other health care fraud.

According to data from HHS-OIG, of those subjects investigated in cases with a judgment or settlement, 275 subjects were to pay restitution as a result of the judgment or settlement and 89 subjects were to pay fines. Approximately 38 percent of the subjects that were to pay restitution were hospitals; 17 percent were medical facilities; and 11 percent were physicians whose affiliation we were unable to determine. Among those subjects that were to pay fines or restitution, or both, the average amounts were about $7.1 million in fines and about $5.4 million in restitution. In total, subjects were to pay over $2.1 billion in combined fines and restitution as a result of the judgments or settlements.[33]

Nearly 2,200 Individuals and Entities Were Excluded from Program Participation by HHS-OIG, about 60 Percent of Whom Were in the Nursing Profession

HHS-OIG excluded individuals and entities from participating in federal health care programs for a variety of reasons in 2010. These reasons included convictions for health care fraud as well as reasons other than for health care fraud, such as patient abuse or neglect.[34] When individuals or entities are excluded, their provider enrollment is revoked and they are not eligible to bill for services provided.[35] According to 2010 exclusion data we received from HHS-OIG, 2,190 individuals and entities were excluded. About 60 percent of the individuals and entities excluded were those in the nursing profession, such as nurses and nurses' aides. The next-largest provider type excluded was pharmacies or individuals affiliated with pharmacies, though they only represented about 7 percent of the 2010 exclusions. (See table 12 for additional information on the types of providers excluded.)

---

[33]According to 2010 data from HHS-OIG, subjects of civil cases were to pay about $633.4 million in fines and $1.474 billion in restitution. HHS-OIG also receives recoveries, which is money returned administratively—such as through self-disclosure, demand letters, or prepayment prior to disposition—rather than settlements or judgments.

[34]As previously noted, HHS-OIG can exclude individuals and entities from program participation for a variety of reasons other than for a health care fraud conviction, including license suspension, surrender, or revocation. The exclusions data we received from HHS-OIG contains all exclusions, not those exclusively related to health care fraud convictions.

[35]Additionally, HHS-OIG has the authority to impose a civil monetary penalty on anyone who employs an excluded individual or entity.

Table 12: Number of Individuals and Entities Excluded from Program Participation, by Provider Type, 2010

Provider type	Exclusions	Percentage
Nursing profession with unknown affiliation	1,281	58.5%
Pharmacies	150	6.8
Health care provider with unknown affiliation	125	5.7
Mental health centers, clinics, or facilities	100	4.6
Medical centers, clinics, or facilities	98	4.5
Durable medical equipment suppliers	85	3.9
Nursing homes	75	3.4
Home health agencies	51	2.3
Other	43	2.0
Other centers, clinics, or facilities	42	1.9
Medical practices	39	1.8
Medical transportation companies	34	1.6
Dental clinics or practices	28	1.3
Government employees, contractors, or grantees	12	0.5
Pharmaceutical manufacturers or suppliers	9	0.4
Hospitals	8	0.4
Management service providers	6	0.3
Insurance companies	3	0.1
Unaffiliated individuals	1	0.0
Total	**2,190**	

Source: GAO analysis of Department of Health and Human Services' Office of Inspector General data.

Notes: Data in this table are for calendar year 2010 and do not include cases also resulting in a civil monetary penalty imposed by HHS-OIG.

There were a number of reasons why the 2,190 individuals and entities were excluded; about 42 percent were excluded for license revocation, suspension, or surrender; over 28 percent were for program-related convictions; and about 10 percent were for felony health care fraud convictions. Most of those excluded because of revoked, suspended, or surrendered licenses were in the nursing profession. (See table 13 for additional information on the reasons for excluding individuals in 2010.)

Table 13: Number of Exclusions from Program Participation by Reason, 2010

Exclusion reasons	Number of exclusions	Percentage
License revocation/suspension/surrender	909	41.5%
Program-related conviction	619	28.3
Felony health care fraud conviction	228	10.4
Patient abuse/neglect conviction	185	8.4
Felony controlled substance conviction	142	6.5
Federal/state health care program exclusion/suspension	35	1.6
Entity owned/controlled by excluded/convicted individual	32	1.5
Conviction relating to program or health care fraud	17	0.8
Fraud/kickbacks	10	0.5
Individual controlling excluded/convicted entity	5	0.2
Obstruction of an investigation conviction	4	0.2
Failure to grant immediate access	2	0.1
Misdemeanor controlled substance conviction	2	0.1
Total	**2,190**	

Source: GAO analysis of Department of Health and Human Services' Office of Inspector General (HHS-OIG) data.

Notes: Data in this table are for calendar year 2010 and do not include cases resulting in a civil monetary penalty imposed by HHS-OIG.

Home Health Providers Were the Largest Percentage of Criminal Convictions for MFCUs, and Pharmaceutical Manufacturers Were Ordered to Pay the Most in Civil Cases

Data we received from 10 state MFCUs show that more than 40 percent of the fraud subjects were home health care providers, and health care practitioners. Home health care providers also accounted for nearly 40 percent of criminal convictions and about 45 percent of subjects sentenced in 2010. In 2010, pharmaceutical manufacturers were to pay more than 60 percent of the total amount of civil judgments and settlements.

More Than 40 Percent of Subjects in Fraud Cases Were Home Health Care Providers and Health Care Practitioners

Of the 2,742 subjects of health care fraud in Medicaid and CHIP referred to MFCUs for investigation, more than 40 percent were affiliated with two provider categories: home health care providers (26.6 percent) and health care practitioners (14.8 percent).[36] Home health care providers and pharmaceutical manufacturers are the two provider categories that experienced the highest increases when comparing 2005 and 2010 data. For example, the number of home health care providers suspected of fraud increased significantly from 2005 to 2010, from 357 subjects to 730, a 104 percent increase. This was primarily driven by an increase in fraud cases among health care aides, which increased from 79 subjects in 2005 to 324 in 2010. Similarly, the number of pharmaceutical manufacturers in fraud cases increased significantly from 71 in 2005 to 296 in 2010. (See table 14, below, for additional information on provider types referred to MFCUs in fraud investigations.)

---

[36]Each instance of fraud in the data submitted by the 10 MFCUs represents one individual, facility, or organization that is referred to as the subject of the fraud case. Fraud case subjects may be an individual, such as a dentist or a nurse; an organization, such as a pharmaceutical manufacturer; or a facility, such as a hospital. Several subjects may be investigated in one fraud case; however, in the 10 states' MFCU data submitted, each subject in a fraud case is counted separately. Home health care providers include home health agencies and home health care aides; and health care practitioners include physicians, doctors of osteopathy, nurses, physician assistants, and nurse practitioners.

Table 14: Number of Subjects of Health Care Fraud Referred to 10 Medicaid Fraud Control Units (MFCU) for Investigation, by Provider Type, 2005 and 2010

	2005		2010	
Provider category	Total number of fraud subjects that were referred for investigation	Percentage of total number of subjects referred	Total number of fraud subjects that were referred for investigation	Percentage of total number of subjects referred
Home health care providers	357	16.4 %	730	26.6%
Health care practitioners	487	22.3	406	14.8
Other health care services	384	17.6	384	14.0
Pharmaceutical manufacturers	71	3.3	296	10.8
Durable medical equipment suppliers	143	6.6	214	7.8
Dentists	125	5.7	184	6.7
Long-term care facilities	111	5.1	157	5.7
Management service providers	211	9.7	148	5.4
Pharmacies	179	8.2	120	4.4
Hospitals and other medical facilities[a]	113	5.2	103	3.8
Total	2,181		2,742	

Source: GAO analysis of state MFCU data submitted by California, Florida, Illinois, Indiana, Louisiana, Massachusetts, New York, Ohio, Texas, and Virginia, October and November 2011.

Notes: Data in this table are for calendar years 2005 and 2010.

Data in this table are for fraud in Medicaid and the Children's Health Insurance Program (CHIP); however, the data may also include some health care fraud cases involving Medicare.

Each instance of fraud in the data submitted by the 10 MFCUs represents one individual, facility, or organization that is referred to as the subject of a fraud case. Fraud subjects may be an individual, such as a dentist or a nurse, an organization such as a pharmaceutical manufacturer, or a facility such as a hospital. Several subjects may be investigated in one fraud case; however, in the MFCU data submitted each subject in a fraud case is counted separately.

Data received from the state MFCUs included information for any actions—such as indictments, convictions, or penalties—that occurred on a subject's fraud case in 2005 or 2010. For example, if a subject was indicted in 2004 and sentenced in 2005, the MFCU data would only include information about the subject's sentencing in 2005, because the indictment occurred in a year outside of our data request.

[a]In this table, hospitals and other medical facilities includes hospitals, radiology services, and substance abuse treatment centers.

Over half of the MFCUs' subjects of fraud cases in 2010 were referred by the states' Medicaid agencies (30.9 percent) and private citizens (25.1 percent). MFCUs do not pursue all cases of health care fraud that are referred to them.

Home Health Providers Accounted for Nearly 40 percent of Criminal Convictions and About 45 Percent of Subjects Sentenced for 2010

Example of a Criminal Health Care Fraud Case Handled by an MFCU

In 2010, several home health care aides were convicted for submitting false time sheets to their employers, either billing for hours that were not worked or billing for services that patients did not need. This caused the home health agency they worked for to submit bills to Medicaid for services the aides did not provide.

In 2010, 692 subjects were indicted or charged in criminal health care fraud cases handled by 10 MFCUs; of those, nearly 40 percent were home health care providers—which includes home health care agencies, and home health care aides. Home health care providers also accounted for nearly 40 percent of criminal fraud convictions in 2010; health care practitioners—physicians, doctors of osteopathy, nurses, physician assistants, and nurse practitioners—had the second-highest percentage of criminal convictions in 2010 with approximately 16 percent. The number of home health care providers convicted in criminal cases more than doubled from 79 convictions in 2005 to 192 convictions in 2010, and health care practitioners had an increase of 11 convictions compared to 2005. (See table 15 for additional information about criminal case outcomes and prosecutions of subjects by provider type for cases handled by 10 MFCUs.)

Table 15: Outcomes for Subjects of Criminal Health Care Fraud Cases Handled by 10 Medicaid Fraud Control Units (MFCU), by Provider Type, 2010

Provider category	Number of subjects				
	Indicted/charged	Convicted	Acquitted	Dismissed	Other results[a]
Home health care providers	271	192	1	6	4
Health care practitioners	95	76	2	9	2
Other health care services	88	73	0	16	3
Management service providers	70	67	0	22	0
Durable medical equipment suppliers	89	46	3	14	2
Pharmacies	27	19	0	6	0
Long-term care facilities	5	7	0	3	0
Dentists	38	5	0	4	1
Hospitals and other medical facilities[b]	9	3	0	2	0
Pharmaceutical manufacturers	0	0	0	2	0
Total	692	488	6	84	12

Source: GAO analysis of state MFCU data submitted by California, Florida, Illinois, Indiana, Louisiana, Massachusetts, New York, Ohio, Texas, and Virginia, October and November 2011.

Notes: Data in this table are for calendar year 2010.

Data in this table are for fraud in Medicaid and the Children's Health Insurance Program (CHIP); however, the data may also include some health care fraud cases involving Medicare.

Each instance of fraud in the data submitted by the 10 MFCUs represents one individual, facility, or organization that is referred to as the subject of a fraud case. Fraud subjects may be an individual, such as a dentist or a nurse, an organization such as a pharmaceutical manufacturer, or a facility such as a hospital. Several subjects may be investigated in one fraud case; however, in the MFCU data submitted each subject in a fraud case is counted separately.

Data received from the state MFCUs included information for any actions—such as indictments, convictions, or penalties—that occurred on a subject's fraud case in 2005 or 2010. For example, if a subject was indicted in 2004 and sentenced in 2005, the MFCU data would only include information about the subject's sentencing in 2005, because the indictment occurred in a year outside of our data request.

[a]This would include subjects whose cases resulted in diversions and other criminal case outcomes that were not included in the convicted column of this table.

[b]In this table, hospitals and other medical facilities includes hospitals, radiology services, and substance abuse treatment centers.

According to 2010 data for cases handled by the 10 MFCUs, home health care providers had the largest number of subjects sentenced to incarceration, probation, or other criminal case outcomes, accounting for nearly 45 percent of the total number of subjects. Durable medical equipment suppliers accounted for the largest monetary penalties, yet had relatively few subjects sentenced to incarceration, probation, or other criminal case outcomes, such as deferred sentences. Of all of the subjects sentenced, 42 percent were sentenced to probation, 32 percent were sentenced to incarceration, and 26 percent received other criminal case outcomes.[37] (See table 16 for additional information on criminal case outcomes.)

Table 16: Criminal Case Sentencing Outcomes for Subjects of Health Care Fraud Cases Handled by 10 Medicaid Fraud Control Units (MFCU), by Provider Type, 2010

Provider category	Number of subjects sentenced to incarceration	Number of subjects sentenced to probation	Number of subjects with other criminal case outcomes	Total number of subjects sentenced	Percent of total number sentenced	Total amounts of monetary penalties ordered to pay[a]	Percent of total monetary penalties ordered to pay
Home health care providers	107	135	121	363	44.5%	$7,471,691	9.6%
Health care practitioners	41	60	23	124	15.2	16,741,992	21.6
Management service providers	45	54	17	116	14.2	10,067,803	13.0
Other health care services	36	50	24	110	13.5	10,162,549	13.1
Durable medical equipment suppliers	25	20	6	51	6.3	25,615,519	33.0
Pharmacies	7	13	11	31	3.8	7,287,855	9.4
Long-term care facilities	2	5	5	12	1.5	22,034	0.03
Dentists	2	3	1	6	0.7	26,760	0.03
Hospitals and other medical facilities[b]	0	1	2	3	0.4	265,308	0.3
Pharmaceutical manufacturers	0	0	0	0	0.0	0	0.0
Total	265	341	210	816		$77,661,510	

Source: GAO analysis of state MFCU data submitted by California, Florida, Illinois, Indiana, Louisiana, Massachusetts, New York, Ohio, Texas, and Virginia, October and November 2011.

Notes: Data in this table are for calendar year 2010.

Data in this table are for fraud in Medicaid and the Children's Health Insurance Program (CHIP); however, the data may also include some health care fraud cases involving Medicare.

Each instance of fraud in the data submitted by the 10 MFCUs represents one individual, facility, or organization that is referred to as the subject of a fraud case. Fraud subjects may be an individual such as a dentist or a nurse, an organization such as a pharmaceutical manufacturer, or a facility such as a hospital. Several subjects may be investigated in one fraud case; however, in the MFCU data submitted each subject in a fraud case is counted separately.

[37]Other criminal case outcomes may include deferred sentences, limits on future employment, or limits on contact with certain individuals.

GAO-12-820 Fraud in Medicare, Medicaid, and CHIP

Data received from the state MFCUs included information for any actions—such as indictments, convictions, or penalties—that occurred on a subject's fraud case in 2005 or 2010. For example, if a subject was indicted in 2004 and sentenced in 2005, the MFCU data would only include information about the subject's sentencing in 2005, because the indictment occurred in a year outside of our data request.

[a]Monetary penalties include subjects being ordered to pay fines, restitution to the Medicaid program, and investigative costs.

[b]In this table, hospitals and other medical facilities includes hospitals, radiology services, and substance abuse treatment centers.

Pharmaceutical Manufacturers Were Ordered to Pay More Than 60 Percent of the Civil Judgments and Settlements in 2010

Example of a Civil Health Care Fraud Case Handled by an MFCU

A pharmaceutical manufacturer agreed to pay a settlement of more than $500 million in 2010 for off-label marketing of a prescription drug. The settlement would reimburse Medicaid and other health care programs for harm suffered by this conduct. The manufacturer promoted the drug for uses that were not approved to primary care physicians in addition to psychiatrists, and for off-label use in children, adolescents and dementia patients. These uses were not medically accepted indications and were uses for which state Medicaid programs would not have approved reimbursement.

In 2010, cases handled by the 10 MFCUs involving pharmaceutical manufacturers resulted in the largest amount of civil judgments and settlements, totaling $509.4 million and representing about 62 percent of all judgments and settlements. According to the 2010 data, 360 subjects were ordered to pay nearly $829 million in civil judgments or settlements. This represents an increase of 71 percent in the number of subjects compared to 2005 when 211 subjects were ordered to pay over $808 million in civil judgments or settlements. In 2010, cases involving home health care providers had the third-highest number of civil judgments and settlements, and the second-lowest amounts of monetary penalties; conversely, there were relatively few management service provider subjects, yet those were the second-highest monetary penalty amounts among the categories of providers. (See table 17 for additional information on civil judgments and settlements by provider type.)

Table 17: Civil Judgments or Settlements for Subjects of Health Care Fraud Cases Handled by 10 Medicaid Fraud Control Units (MFCU) by Provider Type, 2005 and 2010

	2005		2010	
Provider category	Total number of civil judgments or settlements	Total amount defendants ordered to pay (dollars)	Total number of civil judgments or settlements	Total amount defendants ordered to pay (dollars)
Pharmaceutical manufacturers	26	$360,464,411	111	$509,372,944
Other health care services	27	20,653,844	54	81,351,840
Home health care providers	22	15,977,759	43	1,347,230
Health care practitioners	23	7,827,100	33	5,688,174
Management service providers	13	258,291,795	27	129,634,819
Pharmacies	27	52,040,671	24	48,985,438
Hospitals and other medical facilities[a]	23	87,481,318	21	26,872,521
Long-term care facilities	20	1,115,974	18	258,552
Dentists	13	1,466,934	17	9,263,750
Durable medical equipment suppliers	17	2,951,298	12	15,798,274
Total	**211**	**$808,271,103**	**360**	**$828,573,542**

Source: GAO analysis of state MFCU data submitted by California, Florida, Illinois, Indiana, Louisiana, Massachusetts, New York, Ohio, Texas, and Virginia, October and November 2011.

Notes: Data in this table are for calendar years 2005 and 2010.

Data in this table are for fraud in Medicaid and the Children's Health Insurance Program (CHIP); however, the data may also include some health care fraud cases involving Medicare.

Each instance of fraud in the data submitted by the 10 MFCUs represents one individual, facility, or organization that is referred to as the subject of a fraud case. Fraud subjects may be an individual such as a dentist or a nurse, an organization such as a pharmaceutical manufacturer, or a facility such as a hospital. Several subjects may be investigated in one fraud case; however, in the MFCU data submitted each subject in a fraud case is counted separately.

Data received from the state MFCUs included information for any actions—such as indictments, convictions, or penalties—that occurred on a subject's fraud case in 2005 or 2010. For example, if a subject was indicted in 2004 and sentenced in 2005, the MFCU data would only include information about the subject's sentencing in 2005, because the indictment occurred in a year outside of our data request.

[a]In this table, hospitals and other medical facilities includes hospitals, radiology services, and substance abuse treatment centers.

Agency Comments

GAO provided a draft of the report to DOJ and HHS. DOJ provided technical comments, which have been incorporated as appropriate. HHS did not comment on the draft.

As agreed with your offices, unless you publicly announce the contents of this report earlier, we plan no further distribution until 30 days from the report date. At that time, we will send copies to the Secretaries of Health and Human Services and Justice, the Inspector General of HHS, and other interested parties. In addition, the report will be available at no charge on the GAO website at http://www.gao.gov.

If you or your staff have any questions about this report, please contact me at (202) 512-7114 or kingk@gao.gov. Contact points for our Offices of Congressional Relations and Public Affairs may be found on the last page of this report. GAO staff who made key contributions to this report are listed in appendix III.

Kathleen M. King
Director, Health Care

Appendix I: Methodology for Analyzing Data Obtained from the Federal Agencies

To identify subjects of health care fraud cases in Medicare, Medicaid, and the Children's Health Insurance Program (CHIP)—including referrals, investigations, prosecutions, and outcomes—by provider type, and to examine changes in the distribution of provider types in 2005 and 2010, we obtained data on health care fraud cases from the Department of Health and Human Services' Office of Inspector General (HHS-OIG), the Department of Justice's (DOJ) Executive Office of U.S. Attorneys (EOUSA)—which provides administrative support for the 94 U.S. Attorney's Offices (USAO)—and DOJ's Civil Division.[1] We obtained data on fraud cases involving Medicare, Medicaid, and CHIP that were closed in calendar year 2005 or 2010. We collected data for closed cases only—meaning that the agencies were no longer actively investigating or prosecuting a case—to avoid concerns about analyzing or reporting information about open cases.

We obtained data from HHS-OIG's Investigative Reporting and Information System, which contains information on health care fraud cases received or investigated by HHS-OIG. The data we received contained information on civil and criminal health care fraud cases closed in calendar years 2005 or 2010, as well as exclusions from program participation. The HHS-OIG data included information about the subjects, sources of the cases, outcomes of the investigations and prosecutions (if the cases were pursued), and the reasons for which the cases were closed (such as lack of evidence). The data we received from HHS-OIG also contained information on the provider types of the subjects.

Additionally, we obtained data from two divisions within DOJ—EOUSA and the Civil Division. The data we received from EOUSA was from the Legal Information Office Network System and contained information about the subjects of the fraud cases, outcomes of the prosecutions, and the reasons for which the cases were closed. Provider type is not a required field in the USAOs database; consequently the USAOs do not consistently have provider type information. DOJ's Civil Division provided us data from the CASES database. The data received contained

---

[1]Although the Federal Bureau of Investigation (FBI) investigates health care fraud, and DOJ's Criminal Division prosecutes health care fraud, we did not request data from them because officials told us that the FBI and DOJ's Criminal Division primarily work on health care fraud cases jointly with the HHS-OIG or USAOs. Officials indicated that the vast majority of health care fraud cases handled by FBI and DOJ's Criminal Division would be entered in databases used either by HHS-OIG or USAOs.

GAO-12-820 Fraud in Medicare, Medicaid, and CHIP

information about the subjects, outcomes of the fraud cases, and reasons the cases were closed. The DOJ Civil Division does not collect information on the subject's provider type. The data we received from HHS-OIG pertained only to health care fraud in Medicare, Medicaid, and CHIP; however, data we received from the USAOs and DOJ's Civil Division may have also included other federal health care program fraud as well as fraud in the private sector as the databases used to track fraud cases do not capture fraud exclusively in Medicare, Medicaid, and CHIP.

Many fraud cases are handled jointly with HHS-OIG, USAOs, and DOJ's Civil Division, and are entered separately into each agency's database that tracks fraud cases. As a result, the data we received contains duplicate information on health care fraud cases and subjects. In order to minimize the duplication across the data we received, we identified fraud case subjects that were in more than one data set we received by comparing subject information to the extent possible. We then excluded the duplicate data that we identified so that each subject was only included once. However, it is possible that our analysis still includes some duplication in fraud cases and subjects. For cases and subjects that we identified as a match, we used the information in the HHS-OIG data instead of either the USAO data or DOJ's Civil Division data because the HHS-OIG data contained information on the subject's provider type. Among the data involving criminal cases, we identified 590 subjects—291 subjects in the 2005 data and 299 subjects in the 2010 data—that were matches between the HHS-OIG data and the USAO data. For civil case data, we identified 423 subjects—166 subjects in the 2005 data and 257 subjects in the 2010 data—that were matches between data we received from HHS-OIG, the USAOs, or DOJ's Civil Division. We removed the duplicate subjects we identified from parts of our analysis.

In the USAO and Civil Division data, there were 2,470 subjects—1,484 of which were investigated in civil cases, and 986 that were investigated in criminal cases—for which we did not identify a duplicate case in the HHS-OIG data, and did not contain information on the provider type. To identify the type of provider for these subjects, we obtained information from court records using the Public Access to Court Electronic Records (PACER).[2]

---

[2]PACER is an electronic public access service that allows users to obtain case and docket information from federal appellate, district, and bankruptcy courts via the Internet.

We reviewed court documents, such as indictments and plea agreements, to obtain information on the subject's provider type. We reviewed information we found using PACER and categorized it into one of the provider categories in our analysis. However, our analysis of the changes in the types of providers in 2005 and 2010 is limited since the percentage of subjects for which we were unable to determine the provider type was substantially higher in 2005 for civil case subjects. One of the reasons we could not determine the provider type was because many of the court records for 2005 were not available in PACER.

After we identified the provider types for data we received from USAOs and DOJ's Civil Division, and after reviewing the data on provider types in the HHS-OIG data, we created categories of providers in order to analyze the data. We assigned the subjects categories: the entity in which health care was provided, and the subject's role in providing care (if care was provided). For example, an owner of a durable medical equipment supply company was categorized into an entity (durable medical equipment supplier) and a role (management employee); a physician employed by a hospital would be categorized as hospital for the entity and physician for the role. Table 18 provides additional details about the categories we developed for our analysis.

Table 18: Categories of Provider Types Developed for Analysis of Health Care Fraud Case Subjects

Entity	Types of providers included
Dental clinics or practices	Includes dentists, employees, and management who are employed by or operate dental clinics or practices; and entities that are dental clinics or practices.
Durable medical equipment suppliers	Includes employees and management—such as owners and operators—of durable medical equipment suppliers that provide medical equipment and supplies; and entities that are durable medical equipment suppliers themselves. This category includes many types of durable medical equipment such as diabetic supplies, hearing aids, home infusion, oxygen, and power vehicles.
Government employees, contractors, or grantees	Includes employees, contractors, grantees, nurses, management, or state, local, or tribal agencies that are affiliated with a government agency. This category includes federal government employees, government grantees, and contractors who have received government contracts.
Health care providers with unknown affiliation	Includes physicians, physician assistants, nurses, health care aides, and employees whose affiliation we could not determine. This category includes physicians who may specialize in a particular area of medicine, such as cardiology, though we do not know where the physician practices.
Home health agencies	Includes employees, management, nurses, and health care aides who are employed by or operate home health agencies; and entities that are home health agencies themselves.
Hospitals	Includes employees, management, nurses, physicians, and pharmacists who are employed by hospitals; and entities that are hospitals themselves. This category also includes state and local government hospitals.
Individuals with unknown affiliation	Includes individuals and employees that we could not determine if they were health care providers or whether they were affiliated with a medical setting such as a hospital or medical center.
Insurance companies	Includes employees, management, nurses, and health care aides who are employed by or operate health insurance companies; and entities that are insurance companies themselves. This category includes private health insurance companies, health care conglomerates, health-maintenance organizations, and preferred provider organizations.
Management service providers	Includes employees and management who are employed by or operate companies that provide management services, such as billing, accounting, investing, or legal services; and entities that are companies that provide management services.
Medical centers or clinics	Includes employees, management, nurses, physicians, and health care aides who are employed by or operate medical centers, clinics, or facilities; and entities that are medical centers or clinics. This category includes clinics, such as intercare facilities, hospice clinics, and other clinics that specialize in a particular area of medicine.
Medical practices	Includes employees, management, nurses, physicians, and health care aides who are employed by or operate medical practices or medical groups; and entities that are medical practices themselves. This category includes medical practices that specialize in a particular area of medicine, such as cardiology or dermatology.
Medical supply companies	Includes employees and management who are employed by or operate medical supply manufacturers or suppliers; and entities that are medical supply manufacturers or suppliers themselves.
Medical transportation companies	Includes employees and management who are employed by or operate medical transportation companies, such as ambulance companies; and entities that are medical transportation companies themselves.

Entity	Types of providers included
Mental health centers or clinics	Includes employees, management, and nurses who are employed by or operate mental health centers or clinics; and entities that are mental health centers or clinics themselves. This category includes community mental health centers, psychology practices, and counseling centers.
Nursing homes	Includes employees, management, nurses, and health care aides who are employed by or operate nursing homes, such as skilled nursing facilities, adult homes, and boarding homes; and entities that are nursing homes themselves.
Other	Includes private citizens or individuals who were either not health care providers or whose affiliation was unknown.
Other centers, clinics, or facilities	Includes employees, management, nurses, and health care aides who are employed by or operate centers, clinics, and facilities, such as laboratories, physical therapy clinics, and optical practices; and entities themselves. This category includes centers, clinics, and facilities that are not otherwise specified in the other categories such as medical clinics, hospitals, nursing homes, or mental health centers or clinics.
Pharmaceutical manufacturers or suppliers	Includes employees and management who are employed by or operate pharmaceutical manufacturing or supplying companies; and entities that are pharmaceutical manufacturers or suppliers themselves.
Pharmacies	Includes employees, management, and pharmacists who are employed by or operate pharmacies; and entities that are pharmacies themselves.

Source: GAO analysis of data obtained from the Department of Health and Human Services' Office of Inspector General, U.S. Attorney's Offices, and the Department of Justice's Civil Division.

To assess the reliability of the data we received from HHS-OIG, USAOs, and DOJ's Civil Division, we interviewed officials from each of those agencies about the quality of the data, reviewed relevant documentation, and examined the data for reasonableness and internal consistency. We found these data were sufficiently reliable for the purposes of our report.

Appendix II: Methodology for Selecting State Medicaid Fraud Control Units and Analyzing Submitted Data

To identify subjects of Medicaid and Children's Health Insurance Program (CHIP) fraud cases investigated or prosecuted, or both, by Medicaid Fraud Control Units (MFCU) by provider type, and to examine changes in the distribution of provider types investigated and prosecuted for fraud in 2005 and 2010, we collected data from 10 state MFCUs. Using data about MFCUs collected by the Department of Health and Human Services' Office of Inspector General (HHS-OIG), we selected the 10 state MFCUs that collectively accounted for the majority of open fraud investigations, fraud indictments or charges, fraud convictions, MFCU grant expenditures, and number of MFCU staff for all MFCUs in fiscal year 2010. The state MFCUs we selected also represented over 40 percent of the civil settlements and judgments—though we were not able to analyze fraud-specific civil settlements and judgments because the HHS-OIG data available do not separate out fraud settlements and judgments from abuse and neglect case settlements and judgments. The 10 selected MFCUs were in California, Florida, Illinois, Indiana, Louisiana, Massachusetts, New York, Ohio, Texas, and Virginia.[1] The 10 selected MFCUs accounted for 66 percent of MFCU grant expenditures. (See table 19 for additional information about the MFCUs.)

---

[1] We did not receive complete CHIP fraud data from Florida, New York, and Texas because the MFCUs in these states do not investigate fraud in CHIP. In the other seven states, data on CHIP fraud were included.

Table 19: Information about Health Care Fraud Handled by 10 State Medicaid Fraud Control Units (MFCU), Fiscal Year 2010

States	Open fraud investigations	Fraud indictments/ charges	Fraud convictions	Civil settlements/ judgments[a]	MFCU grant expenditures	Number of MFCU staff
California	840	113	104	52	$27,703,377	185
Florida	628	73	54	73	15,629,601	166
Illinois	186	15	23	18	10,063,030	69
Indiana	562	7	14	34	4,250,731	44
Louisiana	276	79	40	30	4,616,945	51
Massachusetts	278	16	4	36	4,710,043	40
New York	588	83	102	124	40,520,980	306
Ohio	457	105	95	42	5,346,883	57
Texas	1,262	128	80	17	16,950,656	183
Virginia	246	11	11	11	5,913,594	70
10-state total	5,323	630	527	437	$135,705,840	1,171
Total of all state MFCUs	9,710	1,048	839	1,077	$205,500,671	1,827.5
Percentage of national total represented by 10 selected MFCUs	54.8	60.1	62.8	40.6	66.0	64.1

Source: GAO analysis of the Department of Health and Human Services' Office of Inspector General (HHS-OIG) MFCU statistical data for fiscal year 2010.

[a]Civil settlements and judgments data may include other cases in addition to health care fraud cases because the available HHS-OIG data includes both fraud cases and abuse and neglect cases.

We collected data from the state MFCUs by developing a standardized data-collection instrument based on the HHS-OIG's Quarterly Statistical MFCU Report Template and accompanying definitions.[2] (See table 20 for additional information about the definitions for the categories of provider types.)

---

[2]MFCUs are required to submit data to the HHS-OIG quarterly regarding the number of investigations, open investigations by provider type, criminal and civil case results, administrative actions ordered, and monetary collections resulting from criminal and civil judgments or settlements.

Table 20: Categories of Provider Types Used in Data Collection Instrument Sent to State Medicaid Fraud Control Units for Analysis of Health Care Fraud Case Subjects

Entity	Types of providers included
Management service providers	Includes managed care organizations, or other entities providing health care on an arranged, prepaid fixed amount; organizations or individuals providing Medicaid program administration support; billing companies that prepare and submit health care claims for payment on behalf of a health care provider or providers; and other program related services.
Dentists	Includes those licensed by the state to provide professional dentistry services to individuals, and partnerships or other formal organization of dentists.
Durable medical equipment suppliers	Includes persons or facilities that sell or lease disposable or nondisposable medical equipment or supplies.
Health care practitioners	Includes physicians and doctors of osteopathy licensed to provide medical care, regardless of specialty, partnerships or other formal physician organizations; and nurses, physician assistants, dental hygienists, and nurse practitioners, and other providers of health care services, not otherwise listed, who are regulated by the state in some manner through professional licensure or registration.
Home health care providers	Includes home health agencies and home health care aides—nonprofessionally licensed individuals providing homemaker, housekeeping, or personal services to individuals, that are reimbursed by federally-funded health care programs. May also include in-home care providers, personal care aides, and relative care givers.
Hospitals and other medical facilities	Includes hospitals; radiology—a person or organization (other than radiologists, who would be reported as physicians) who provides X-ray, MRI, or other radiology imaging services; and substance abuse treatment centers.
Nursing homes	Includes all nursing facilities, licensed to provide skilled or intermediate care for individuals age 21 years or older, and other long-term care facilities such as those residential settings that provide nursing or personal care services for residents, regardless of age.
Other health care services	Includes podiatrists, optometrists and opticians, chiropractors, other practitioners, labs, mental health centers, clinics and facilities, including counselors and psychologists, and medical transportation providers.
Pharmaceutical manufacturers	Includes manufacturers of medicines/controlled substances that bill to federally funded health care programs.
Pharmacies	Includes a person or organization operating a facility where medicine is compounded and dispensed, including pharmacists.

Source: GAO analysis of Department of Health and Human Services' Office of Inspector General documents.

Before finalizing the data-collection instrument, we asked officials from two MFCUs to review the instrument to determine if the instrument would elicit appropriate responses, and to identify any data that would be particularly challenging for a MFCU to provide. We also interviewed officials from the Centers for Medicare & Medicaid Services, the HHS-OIG's Office of Evaluation and Inspections, and the National Association of MFCUs to obtain information on fraud cases handled by the MFCUs.

We collected data for closed health care fraud cases only—meaning that agencies were no longer actively investigating or prosecuting a case—to avoid concerns about analyzing or reporting information about open cases. We requested data from the state MFCUs for any actions—such as indictments, convictions, or penalties—that occurred on a subject's fraud case in 2005 or 2010. For example, if a subject was indicted in 2004 and sentenced in 2005, the MFCU data would only include information about the subject's sentencing in 2005, because the indictment occurred in a year outside of our data request. We requested aggregate subject-level data, rather than case-level data, from the MFCUs using a standardized data-collection instrument.[3] The MFCUs reported information on the total number of fraud subjects they investigated and prosecuted, and did not provide detailed information for each instance of fraud. Because the state MFCUs may work together on certain cases that cross state lines, it is possible that duplicate data are included in our analysis. We relied on the data as reported by the 10 MFCUs and did not independently verify these data. However, we reviewed the data for reasonableness and followed up with state officials for clarification when necessary. We found that these data were sufficiently reliable for the purposes of our report.

---

[3]Each instance of fraud in the data submitted by the 10 MFCUs represents one individual, facility, or organization that is referred to as the subject of the fraud case. Fraud case subjects may be an individual such as a dentist or a nurse, an organization such as a pharmaceutical manufacturer, or a facility such as a hospital. Several subjects may be investigated in one fraud case; however, in the 10 states' MFCU data each subject in a fraud case is counted separately.

GAO-12-820 Fraud in Medicare, Medicaid, and CHIP

Appendix III: GAO Contact and Staff Acknowledgments

GAO Contact	Kathleen M. King, (202) 512-7114 or kingk@gao.gov
Staff Acknowledgments	In addition to the contact named above, key contributors to this report were Martin T. Gahart, Assistant Director; Christie Enders; Jawaria Gilani; Dan Lee; Drew Long; Dawn Nelson; and Monica Perez-Nelson.